Life-transforming truth

life transforming truth

An introduction to the doctrines of grace

William E. Payne

Joshua Press Inc., Ontario, Canada
www.joshuapress.com

Distributed by Sola Scriptura Ministries International
www.sola-scriptura.ca

Editorial director: Michael A.G. Haykin

National Library of Canada Cataloguing in Publication Data

Payne, William E., 1938–1997
Life-transforming truth: an introduction to the doctrines of grace

Includes bibliographical references.
ISBN 1-894400-11-9

1. Grace (Theology). 2. Calvinism. I. Title

BT761.2.P39 2001 234 C2001-930036-0

Dedicated to the glory of our God and Saviour,
with the desire that His greatness in salvation
will be more fully known, and with grateful
thanks to Him for the life and ministry of
our dear pastor and friend, William E. Payne

Contents

Foreword by Carl Muller		9
Introduction		13
1	Understanding depravity	17
2	Rejoicing in election	23
3	Affirming particular redemption	29
4	Effectual calling	35
5	Explaining perseverance	41
6	Exploring regeneration	47
7	Declaring justification	53
8	Experiencing sanctification	59
9	The privilege of adoption	65
10	The hope of glorification	71
Further reading		75

Foreword

The bride eyes not her garment,
But her dear bridegroom's face;
I will not gaze at glory,
But on my King of grace,
Not at the crown He giveth,
But on His piercèd hand:
The Lamb is all the glory
Of Immanuel's land.[1]

This stanza of Anne Cousin's hymn was quoted during the funeral service of Bill Payne, which took place on July 5, 1997. Bill now gazes upon Immanuel's face and he knows with an even greater certainty than he did during the time he was with us that these "doctrines of grace" are not only true, but are to be treasured by the church, and to be trumpeted from her pulpits.

Those of us who had the privilege of knowing Pastor William E. Payne and of sitting under his ministry, will recognize in this book some of the hallmarks of that ministry:

- a thoroughly biblical approach
- startling clarity of thought and expression
- a love for truth and the God of truth
- a solid commitment to the proclamation

[1] By Anne R. Cousin (1824–1906), from her hymn "The Sands of Time"

of the whole counsel of God

- the warmth of a man who unfailingly held "the doctrines of grace with the grace of the doctrines."

Evangelicalism in North America suffers from, among other things, theological anemia. The line between truth and error is blurred, theological distinctives are considered inconsequential, the pulpit has become the focal point of commitment to entertainment, and the faithful ministry of the Word of God is often a thing of the past. Under God, Bill Payne laboured to stem the tide of such folly and to restore, at least in the corner of the vineyard where he served, solid biblical teaching to its rightful place in the Church of Jesus Christ. "Preach the word," was the clarion call of the Apostle Paul. Bill Payne's ministry was an obedient response to that call, and in this book he still speaks.

The second half of the twentieth century has seen a resurgence of the understanding and appreciation of Calvinistic distinctives. Bill Payne was at the forefront of that movement here in Canada (and in Ontario in particular). Those who knew him deeply appreciated the warmth with which he proclaimed the doctrines of grace and the fervour with which he practiced them in his life. In the pulpit, in the classroom, in the living room, Bill was a man mastered by the Sovereign Lord. In this book we see some of the fruit of his walk with God.

I heartily commend this book. It will be useful for those who are struggling with the wonderful truth of God's sovereign grace. It will surely strengthen those who love these doctrines and bring greater clarity to their understanding of them. It will most certainly move the reader to bow, with a sense of wonder, love and praise, before the God of all grace! May our Lord use it for His glory.

Carl Muller

Trinity Baptist Church, Burlington, Ontario, 2001

Introduction

Inevitably names are attached to different churches or groups of Christians. Some are described as Pentecostal or Charismatic, others as Presbyterians, others as Baptists and so on. This does not mean that these groups have nothing in common, nor that among themselves they agree on every detail. The name usually indicates that there is something distinctive to which the group is committed—a particular practice or a particular doctrine or set of doctrines. Now, I refer to myself as a Baptist, but I usually qualify this by calling myself a Reformed Baptist, or Sovereign Grace Baptist, or Calvinistic Baptist. Why is that? Well, for the simple reason that I am a Baptist who is committed to certain doctrines which are often referred to as "the doctrines of grace." Sometimes they are called "the five points of Calvinism." On occasion they may be called "Calvinistic distinctives." There is a historical context to these doctrines that relates to the sixteenth-century Reformation and its aftermath, but I shall not go into that in this book.[1] I believe these doctrines, not because of their historical connection, but because I believe them to be thoroughly biblical.

1 For a good introduction to the sixteenth-century Reformation, see R. Tudur Jones, *The Great Reformation. A wide-ranging survey of the beginnings of Protestantism* (1985 ed.; repr. Bryntirion, Bridgend: Bryntirion Press, 1997). For biographical sketches of some of the leading figures in the Reformation, see Christopher Catherwood, *Five Leading Reformers* (Fearn, Ross-shire: Christian Focus, 2000).

2 Peter 3:15,16
...and consider *that* the longsuffering of our Lord *is* salvation—as also our beloved brother Paul, according to the wisdom given to him, has written to you, as also in all his epistles, speaking in them of these things, in which are some things hard to understand, which untaught and unstable *people* twist to their own destruction, as *they do* also the rest of the Scriptures.

Peter said that there were some things in Paul's writings which were hard to understand (2 Peter 3:15,16), and there are aspects of the doctrines of grace which are hard to understand. The crucial question however is not "are there difficult elements about these doctrines"? but rather "are these doctrines Biblical; are they taught in the Word of God"? The doctrines of grace are humbling doctrines and they often evoke strong reaction in sinful human hearts. Some of us who now rejoice in them can remember when we strongly opposed them! But they are God-honouring doctrines. They are life-transforming doctrines. They are the mega-vitamins needed by a weak and ailing Christian church. Once grasped and understood they will be a mighty blessing to you, for they will reveal the glory of salvation as nothing else can.

Psalm 119:130
The entrance of Your words gives light;
It gives understanding to the simple.

Two things need to be added. The doctrines of grace are not the only doctrines in the Bible. Other great Bible truths must also be held by us to complement and balance them. In this book I hope to deal also with some of these other great doctrines. May the entrance of God's words give light (Psalm 119:130). Further, I encourage you to look up the many Scripture references given in this book and to seek an ever deeper knowledge of the great truths of God's Word.

W.E. Payne

Trinity Baptist Church, Burlington, Ontario, 1996

The source and fount of our salvation
Is the Lord's electing love;
All would suffer condemnation
Were it not for God above.

It was that God enthroned and sovereign
Who decreed to save my soul;
'Twas His everlasting mercy
Which reclaimed and made me whole.

No not in us is found the reason
Why we have in heaven a place;
But in His eternal purpose,
In His free unchanging grace.

Then to the Lord be all the honour,
Give not praise to human will;
Were it not for God's election
We'd be in our bondage still.

William E. Payne (1938–1997)

Perhaps you have thought but little of your state as a lost sinner before [God]; yet you have sufficient proof in your own experience of the degeneracy and dreadful corruption of your nature. Have you learned from it this important lesson? If you have, while you bewail it before God, with shame and self-abhorrence, you will embrace the refuge set before you in the gospel.

Andrew Fuller (1754–1815)
—from a letter to the son of a friend

1 Understanding depravity

Its importance

Romans 3:23
...for all have sinned and fall short of the glory of God.

If we fail to understand the Biblical teaching on this doctrine our understanding of all the doctrines related to salvation will be faulty. To have a right understanding in this matter is therefore crucial. Our understanding of the problem with humanity will govern our understanding of the treatment needed.

To what does the expression refer?

The expression "total depravity" describes the condition of man *as he is now in sin*, as a result of the "Fall" in Adam. It does not indicate man's original state when first created.

What it *does not* mean

It does not mean that every man is as evil as he possibly could be. It does not mean that man is incapable of things considered good and noble from a human viewpoint.

What it *does* mean

Basically it means that sin has affected every aspect of man's being. It means that *in and of himself*, man in the state of sin is unable to do anything that is spiritually good or that will contribute toward his return to and reconciliation with God.

Broadly speaking we may view "man" as comprised of *mind* (intellect, that part of us which thinks and understands); *affections* (that part of us which "feels," either attracting us to something or repelling us from it); and *will* (the volitional part which chooses and acts).

Romans 8:5
For those who live according to the flesh set their minds on the things of the flesh, but those *who live* according to the Spirit, the things of the Spirit.

How has sin affected these basic elements of man's being?

2 Corinthians 4:4
...whose minds the god of this age has blinded, who do not believe, lest the light of the gospel of the glory of Christ, who is the image of God, should shine on them.

1) *The mind has become darkened with respect to spiritual things*
(1 Corinthians 2:14; Romans 8:5;
2 Corinthians 4:4; Ephesians 4:17,18;
Colossians 1:21)

Jeremiah 17:9
"The heart *is* deceitful above all *things*,
And desperately wicked;
Who can know it?"

2) *The affections have been corrupted by sin*
(John 3:19; Job 15:14–16; Genesis 6:5;
Jeremiah 17:9; Mark 7:21,23; Isaiah 59:2)

John 5:40,43,44
"But you are not willing to come to Me that you may have life....I have come in My Father's name, and you do not receive Me; if another comes in his own name, him you will receive. How can you believe, who receive honor from one another, and do not seek the honor that *comes* from the only God?"

3) *The will is in bondage to sin*
(John 5:40,43,44; 6:44; Job 14:4;
Jeremiah 13:23)

It is important to appreciate that the will is controlled by the nature. What we do is determined by what we are, just as the fruit of a tree depends on the nature of the tree. The will is not an independent principle, but is always governed by other elements of the nature.

Jeremiah 13:23
Can the Ethiopian change his skin or the leopard its spots? *Then* may you also do good who are accustomed to do evil.

Consider a sheep and a vulture in a field of grass in which there is the carcass of a dead dog. The sheep will eat the grass. The vulture will eat the dog. Why? Simply because their choice is governed by their nature. Will man then, with darkened mind and corrupted affections, choose Christ and the way of holiness if left to his own free will? No! The faculty of choice is still his and no one coerces him, but, governed by his sinful nature and left to himself, he always makes the wrong choice in spiritual matters. Note especially how this truth is taught in Romans 3:10–18.

Romans 3:10–18
As it is written: "There is none righteous, no, not one; There is none who understands; There is none who seeks after God. They have all turned aside; They have together become unprofitable; There is none who does good, no, not one." "Their throat *is* an open tomb; With their tongues they have practiced deceit"; "The poison of asps *is* under their lips"; "Whose mouth *is* full of cursing and bitterness." "Their feet *are* swift to shed blood; Destruction and misery *are* in their ways; And the way of peace they have not known." "There is no fear of God before their eyes."

Man is invited, and indeed commanded, to repent and believe the gospel. It is his responsibility and duty to do so. He cannot be saved unless he repents of sin and exercises faith in Jesus Christ. Yet, due to his sinful state he is, of himself, unable to do so. This is the alarming condition of a sinner. His need is for a supernatural divine work in his life.

This is confirmed by the way the Bible explains the reception of Christ by some (John 1:12,13).

John 1:12,13
But as many as received Him, to them He gave the right to become children of God, to those who believe in His name: who were born, not of blood, nor of the will of the flesh, nor of the will of man, but of God.

The Bible clearly states what man, by his own will or power, cannot do

- he cannot see the kingdom of God (John 3:3)
- he cannot please God (Romans 8:8)
- he cannot know the things of God (1 Corinthians 2:14)
- he cannot say that Jesus is Lord (as being genuine and real to him) (1 Corinthians 12:3)
- he cannot come to Christ (John 6:44)

Romans 8:8
So then, those who are in the flesh cannot please God.

John 6:44
"No one can come to Me unless the Father who sent Me draws him; and I will raise him up at the last day."

Divine initiative and divine sovereignty

The imagery by which the Bible describes the work of salvation emphasizes the divine initiative and divine sovereignty in this work:

- it is a resurrection (a spiritual resurrection) (Ephesians 2:5,6)
- it is a new creation (2 Corinthians 5:17)
- it is a regeneration (being born again) (John 3:3,5)
- it is a shining of light into darkness (2 Corinthians 4:6)
- it is a taking away the stony heart and the giving of a new heart and a new spirit (Ezekiel 36:26,27).

2 Corinthians 4:6
For it is the God who commanded light to shine out of darkness, who has shone in our hearts to *give* the light of the knowledge of the glory of God in the face of Jesus Christ.

Ezekiel 36:26,27
"I will give you a new heart and put a new spirit within you; I will take the heart of stone out of your flesh and give you a heart of flesh. I will put My Spirit within you and cause you to walk in My statutes, and you will keep My judgments and do *them*."

Man is indeed totally depraved. He is lost in every terrible sense of the word. His desperate need is a supernatural work of God's grace in his soul, to enlighten his mind, to re-order his affections and liberate his will, so that he might understand the gospel and desire and choose Jesus Christ.

The doctrines of our election, and free justification in Christ Jesus, are daily more and more pressed upon my heart. They fill my soul with a holy fire, and afford me great confidence in God my Saviour. Surely I am safe, because put into his almighty arms, though I may fall, yet I shall not utterly be cast away. The Spirit of the Lord Jesus will hold, and uphold me.

George Whitefield (1714–1770)
—from a letter written in 1739

2 Rejoicing in election

The fact of election

What do we mean by the doctrine of election? We mean that out of the ruined mass of fallen humanity Almighty God has chosen a people, a great innumerable company, which he intends to bring to salvation in and through Jesus Christ.

It is one of the most prominent doctrines of Scripture. The whole of the Old Testament is based upon the fact of election. God chose the nation of Israel to be his own possession and passed by other nations. In the New Testament, words indicating this doctrine are used continually (i.e. elect, chosen, ordained).

The election taught in the Bible is seen to be:

1) *Personal*
   (2 Thessalonians 2:13; Colossians 3:12; John 15:16; 2 Peter 1:10)
2) *A sovereign work of God*
   (Ephesians 1:5,11; Romans 9:15,16; Matthew 11:25,26)
3) *Unconditional*
   (Acts 13:48; John 6:37; 10:26–28)
4) *Eternal*
   (Ephesians 1:4; 2 Timothy 1:9; Jeremiah 31:3)

Romans 9:15,16
For He says to Moses, "I will have mercy on whomever I will have mercy, and I will have compassion on whomever I will have compassion." So then *it is* not of him who wills, nor of him who runs, but of God who shows mercy.

Acts 13:48
Now when the Gentiles heard this, they were glad and glorified the word of the Lord. And as many as had been appointed to eternal life believed.

Jeremiah 31:3
The LORD has appeared of old to me, *saying*: "Yes, I have loved you with an everlasting love; Therefore with lovingkindness I have drawn you.

Ephesians 1:4
...just as He chose us in Him before the foundation of the world, that we should be holy and without blame before Him in love.

5) *In Christ*
(Ephesians 1:4)

The background to election

It is vital that we see election against the background of the Fall. It is because this is overlooked or not understood that election is often thought of as "unfair." God is not now dealing with a race of innocents, but a race of rebels and sinners, all of whom deserve eternal damnation. God would be perfectly just to punish all with eternal damnation. However, he has decided to save some out of the fallen race that his grace and mercy might be displayed in them.

God is not obliged to save any. Rather than being criticized for not saving all, he is to be adored for saving any at all! To think that more people would be in heaven were it not for the decree of election is to totally misunderstand Biblical teaching. The fact is that none would be in heaven were it not for God's election.

Total depravity (brought about by man's own sin) has rendered humanity in such a condition (see Chapter 1) that when left to themselves men spurn the invitation of the gospel. Were it not for the intervention of sovereign grace all would perish, and all would deserve to perish. When seen in this light election becomes a precious truth, a cause for praise. The root cause of a man's salvation is the electing grace of God (Romans

Ezekiel 18:20
"The soul who sins shall die. The son shall not bear the guilt of the father, nor the father bear the guilt of the son. The righteousness of the righteous shall be upon himself, and the wickedness of the wicked shall be upon himself.

9:16). The root cause of a man's damnation is his own sin (Ezekiel 18:20).

The results of election

Sometimes human reaction to this teaching of the Scriptures is that if this is true then why preach the gospel, why exhort people to repent and believe? This response is seen to be invalid when we understand that God has not merely chosen people for salvation, but he has ordained that they should be saved through the gospel, through repentance, faith, obedience and holiness: 1 Peter 1:2; 2 Thessalonians 2:13,14; Ephesians 1:4.

No one has grounds for claiming to be saved unless they have exercised repentance toward God and faith in our Lord Jesus Christ, and have begun to walk in the path of discipleship. Paul said that he *knew* that the Thessalonians were elect (1 Thessalonians 1:4) but notice how he knew it (1 Thessalonians 1:5–10). And observe that Romans 9 with its strong teaching on the sovereignty of divine election is followed by Romans 10 with its free offer of the gospel.

No one who has truly repented of their sins, trusted in Christ for salvation, and who is now endeavouring by God's grace to live a life of obedience to him need fear that they are not elect. The fact that these fruits are in the life is the evidence that they are elect. On the other hand, let no one boast that they are the Lord's and elect of God if these fruits

2 Thessalonians 2:13,14
But we are bound to give thanks to God always for you, brethren beloved by the Lord, because God from the beginning chose you for salvation through sanctification by the Spirit and belief in the truth, to which He called you by our gospel, for the obtaining of the glory of our Lord Jesus Christ.

1 Thessalonians 1:4–10
...knowing, beloved brethren, your election by God. For our gospel did not come to you in word only, but also in power, and in the Holy Spirit and in much assurance, as you know what kind of men we were among you for your sake. And you became followers of us and of the Lord, having received the word in much affliction, with joy of the Holy Spirit, so that you became examples to all in Macedonia and Achaia who believe. For from you the word of the Lord has sounded forth, not only in Macedonia and Achaia, but also in every place. Your faith toward God has gone out, so that we do not need to say anything. For they themselves declare concerning us what manner of entry we had to you, and how you turned to God from idols to serve the living and true God, and to wait for His Son from heaven, whom He raised from the dead, *even* Jesus who delivers us from the wrath to come.

2 Timothy 2:19
Nevertheless the solid foundation of God stands, having this seal: "The Lord knows those who are His," and, "Let everyone who names the name of Christ depart from iniquity."

1 John 3:23
And this is His commandment: that we should believe on the name of His Son Jesus Christ and love one another, as He gave us commandment.

John 3:16
"For God so loved the world that He gave His only begotten Son, that whoever believes in Him should not perish but have everlasting life."

are not evident in the life (2 Timothy 2:19).

The effects of election

When a Christian rightly understands this truth it will produce:

- great brokenness and humility before God
- a quickening of his love and adoration of God
- encouragement in the service of God (Acts 16:9,10)

Is election a discouragement to those who wish to be saved?

It should not be; it need not be.

1) *This doctrine does not contradict or cancel the invitations of the gospel. God always keeps his promises.*
(Acts 16:31; John 6:37; Matthew 11:28,29; John 3:36)
2) *The warrant of faith (the basis of our believing in Christ) is not a knowledge of our personal election, but the invitations and commands of God to come to Christ*
(Deuteronomy 29:29; 1 John 3:23)
3) *The invitations of the gospel are expressed in such a way that no person need feel excluded.*
(John 3:16; Romans 10:13)
4) *Where there is a desire to be saved, there is evidence that the Holy Spirit is at work. But don't let it stop there!*

Additional note

Some feel that election must be explained by

the word "foreknowledge" as used in Romans 8:29 and 1 Peter 1:2. The idea is that God elected those whom he knew would respond to the gospel when it was offered to them. A little thought, however, will reveal that we would then not have a doctrine of election but a doctrine of "ratification" (i.e. God choosing those who chose themselves).

Furthermore, the word "foreknowledge" cannot be interpreted this way because:

- it is contrary to the rest of Scripture which clearly states that believing is a result of election (Acts 13:48; John 6:37);
- Romans 8:29 and 1 Peter 1:2 do not speak of "what" God foreknew (i.e. something about them; what they did), but "whom" he foreknew. That is, God does something with respect to *them*;
- repentance and faith are spoken of in the Scriptures as God's gift to his people: Ephesians 2:8; Acts 11:17;
- the word "know" is often used in the Bible of loving (Genesis 4:1; Amos 3:2; Matthew 7:23). To foreknow, therefore, in Romans 8:29 and 1 Peter 1:2 means to "love beforehand."

Acts 13:48
Now when the Gentiles heard this, they were glad and glorified the word of the Lord. And as many as had been appointed to eternal life believed.

Romans 8:29
For whom He foreknew, He also predestined *to be* conformed to the image of His Son, that He might be the firstborn among many brethren.

Ephesians 2:8
For by grace you have been saved through faith, and that not of yourselves; *it is* the gift of God.

Bearing shame and scoffing rude,
In my place condemned He stood;
Sealed my pardon with His blood:
Hallelujah! what a Saviour!

Philip B. Bliss (1838–1876)
—from his hymn "Man of Sorrows! What a Name"

3 Affirming particular redemption

This third distinctive of Calvinism teaches that Christ offered himself on the cross not for every person without exception, but specifically for the elect given to him by the Father. It might be put this way: did Christ die to make the salvation of all merely possible, or did he die to render the salvation of his elect certain? It clarifies the issue to put the focus not on the *extent* of the atonement (for how many?) but on the *intent* (for what purpose?).

Isaiah 53:11,12
He shall see the labor of His soul, *and* be satisfied. By His knowledge My righteous Servant shall justify many, For He shall bear their iniquities. Therefore I will divide Him a portion with the great, And He shall divide the spoil with the strong, Because He poured out His soul unto death, And He was numbered with the transgressors, And He bore the sin of many, And made intercession for the transgressors.

Those who believe that Christ died redemptively for all without exception believe in what is called "universal redemption." Those who believe that Christ died redemptively only for the elect believe in what is termed "particular redemption" or "limited atonement."

Some difficulties posed by "universal redemption"

1) *It presents a redemption that does not really redeem; an atonement that does not atone; a ransom that does not actually set free.*
2) *It presents Christ's work on the cross as a partial failure, for if Christ died with the intent and purpose of saving every person*

without exception then he has manifestly failed.

3) *It does not do justice to the Word of God, for the Bible does not present Christ's death as something which merely makes salvation possible, but as something which actually saves.*
4) *It does a disservice to the justice of God, for it suggests that Christ has been punished for the sins of those who are in hell and who are therefore being punished for their sins. God therefore exacts punishment for their sins twice—first in Christ and then in them.*

Matthew 20:28
"...just as the Son of Man did not come to be served, but to serve, and to give His life a ransom for many."

Hebrews 9:28
...so Christ was offered once to bear the sins of many. To those who eagerly wait for Him He will appear a second time, apart from sin, for salvation.

Ephesians 5:25
Husbands, love your wives, just as Christ also loved the church and gave Himself for her.

Matthew 1:21
"And she will bring forth a Son, and you shall call His name JESUS, for He will save His people from their sins."

1 Timothy 1:15
This *is* a faithful saying and worthy of all acceptance, that Christ Jesus came into the world to save sinners, of whom I am chief.

Galatians 3:13
Christ has redeemed us from the curse of the law, having become a curse for us (for it is written, "Cursed *is* everyone who hangs on a tree").

Hebrews 9:12
Not with the blood of goats and calves, but with His own blood He entered the Most Holy Place once for all, having obtained eternal redemption.

Scriptures which indicate a "limit" on those for whom Christ died

Isaiah 53:11,12; Matthew 20:28; Matthew 26:28; Hebrews 9:28

Scriptures which indicate that the "many" are a definite group

John 10:11,15, 26; Acts 20:28; Ephesians 5:25; Matthew 1:21

Scriptures which indicate the purpose of Christ's coming and death

Matthew 1:21; Luke 19:10; 1 Timothy 1:15; 1 Peter 3:18

Scriptures that indicate what Christ's death actually accomplished

Romans 5:10; Galatians 3:13; Hebrews 9:12

Taken together, these various verses indicate

that Christ came not just to make the salvation of sinners possible but to actually save them. Not just to make sinners "redeemable," but to actually redeem them. Not just to make them "reconcilable," but to actually reconcile them. That this is not the state of all people would indicate that not all were the objects of Christ's atoning work, unless we are prepared to accept that his mission was less than successful.

The faith by which a sinner becomes a partaker of Christ's salvation is itself the gift of God (Ephesians 2:8,9). It is part of the salvation purchased by Christ for his people. That is why the Bible can speak in terms of a real, definite atonement; an atonement that actually atones, a redemption that actually redeems, a ransom that actually sets the prisoner free. For when Christ died he purchased all that was necessary to "bring to God" all those for whom he died (Hebrews 7:25). This included the grace of repentance and faith and the gift of the Spirit.

Hebrews 7:25
Therefore He is also able to save to the uttermost those who come to God through Him, since He always lives to make intercession for them.

The significance of the terms used of Christ's atonement

1) *Redemption*

This means the delivery from captivity and misery by the intervention of a price or ransom. (Matthew 20:28)

2) *Reconciliation*

This means the renewing of friendship between parties previously hostile. (Colossians 1:21,22)

Colossians 1:21,22
And you, who once were alienated and enemies in your mind by wicked works, yet now He has reconciled in the body of His flesh through death, to present you holy, and blameless, and above reproach in His sight.

1 John 4:10
In this is love, not that we loved God, but that He loved us and sent His Son *to be* the propitiation for our sins.

Titus 2:14
...who gave Himself for us, that He might redeem us from every lawless deed and purify for Himself *His* own special people, zealous for good works.

Isaiah 53:5,6
But He *was* wounded for our transgressions, *He was* bruised for our iniquities; The chastisement for our peace *was* upon Him, And by His stripes we are healed. All we like sheep have gone astray; We have turned, every one, to his own way; And the LORD has laid on Him the iniquity of us all.

3) *Propitiation*

This means the turning away of wrath by means of an offering. In the Bible it is used of reconciling to, appeasing and pacifying God in his aversion to sin. (1 John 4:10)

4) *"Dying for us"*

The Greek prepositions "hyper" and "anti," usually translated "for" or "instead of," clearly imply substitution. (Romans 5:8; Galatians 1:4; Titus 2:14; Matthew 20:28)

At the heart of the biblical doctrine of the atonement is the idea of substitution. "He *was* wounded for our transgressions, He *was* bruised for our iniquities...the Lord has laid on Him the iniquity of us all" (Isaiah 53:5,6).

True substitution and universal redemption cannot exist together. One or the other has to go! As the great Puritan author John Owen (1616–1683) put it:

> Either Christ died for:
> - all the sins of all men; or
> - some of the sins of all men; or
> - all the sins of some men

Only one of these statements can be true!

But does not the Bible speak of Christ dying for "all" and for "the world"?

It does indeed; but the following points need to be remembered:

1) *The word "world" is frequently used in the Bible to speak of large numbers.*

(John 12:19; 1 John 5:19)

2) *The term "world" is also used to emphasize the universal aspect of the Christian mission as opposed to the ethnic narrowness of Jewish nationalism.* (John 3:16; 11:50,52; 1 John 2:2)

3) *The term "all" is often used to speak of all without distinction rather than all without exception.* (John 12:32; 1 John 2:2; 1 Timothy 2:6)

John 12:19
The Pharisees therefore said among themselves, "You see that you are accomplishing nothing. Look, the world has gone after Him!"

1 John 2:2
And He Himself is the propitiation for our sins, and not for ours only but also for the whole world.

1 Timothy 2:6
...who gave Himself a ransom for all, to be testified in due time...

What is the practical relevance of this doctrine?

- it magnifies the work of Christ
- it gives hope in evangelism
- it ministers gloriously to a believer's assurance
- it deepens the believer's love for his Lord
- it enables us to offer to sinners a truly finished work

Effectual calling is the work of God's Spirit, whereby, convincing us of our sin and misery, enlightening our minds in the knowledge of Christ, and renewing our wills, he persuades and enables us to embrace Jesus Christ freely offered to us in the gospel.

Westminster Shorter Catechism (1647)
—answer to Question 31

4 Effectual calling

This doctrine has to do with the work of the Holy Spirit in salvation. Although the salvation of God's elect had been secured and purchased by the blood of Christ it was necessary for this salvation to be applied to them, so that they might come into personal possession of that salvation. Bringing the elect to a reception of those blessings in Christ is the work of the Holy Spirit.

The general call and the effectual call

Scripture distinguishes between what has been termed the "general" or "universal" call of the gospel and the "effectual" call.

The general call of the gospel can be rejected and indeed is rejected by men and women because of their sinful state. This call is seen in verses such as Isaiah 45:22; Matthew 11:28; and Isaiah 55:1. This call is genuine and real and is to be issued by God's servants to all mankind. However, the response to this call is illustrated in the parable of the wedding feast in Matthew 22:1–6, where *none* of those invited to the wedding accepted the invitation.

Isaiah 45:22
"Look to Me, and be saved, All you ends of the earth! For I *am* God, and *there is* no other.

Matthew 11:28
"Come to Me, all *you* who labor and are heavy laden, and I will give you rest."

But there is in Scripture also an effectual

Hebrews 9:15
And for this reason He is the Mediator of the new covenant, by means of death, for the redemption of the transgressions under the first covenant, that those who are called may receive the promise of the eternal inheritance.

Jude 1
Jude, a bondservant of Jesus Christ, and brother of James, To those who are called, sanctified by God the Father, and preserved in Jesus Christ.

John 6:37,39
"All that the Father gives Me will come to Me, and the one who comes to Me I will by no means cast out. ...This is the will of the Father who sent Me, that of all He has given Me I should lose nothing, but should raise it up at the last day."

Hebrews 2:13
And again: "I will put My trust in Him." And again: "Here am I and the children whom God has given Me."

Daniel 4:35
All the inhabitants of the earth *are* reputed as nothing; He does according to His will in the army of heaven And *among* the inhabitants of the earth. No one can restrain His hand Or say to Him, "What have You done?"

call. This is a call that not only invites and summons but that also carries with it the power to ensure the desired response. The effectual call not only invites sinners to salvation, but it actually brings them to it. In this call the Holy Spirit makes the general call effectual. It comes through the gospel message to the elect of God in the power of the Holy Spirit (1 Thessalonians 1:4,5).

It is the effectual call to which the Bible refers most often when it speaks of "call," "called," and "calling" (Romans 8:28–30; 1 Corinthians 1:23–27; Hebrews 9:15).

It is in light of this use of the word "call" that the Bible uses the term "called" to describe Christians (Romans 1:6,7; 1 Corinthians 1:9; Jude 1).

The effectual call is the result of God's purpose

To speak of God "trying" to convert people and the Holy Spirit vainly struggling to achieve a goal he longs for but being frustrated and defeated by the unwillingness of men is to present a pathetic and pitiable God unknown in the Bible. The Bible clearly teaches that all those given to Christ in the will and purpose of the Father will be brought to Him in salvation (compare John 6:37,39; 17:2; Hebrews 2:13).

The Bible distinctly says that God's purposes will most certainly come to pass (Daniel 4:35; Isaiah 46:10,11; Job 23:13,14). It is with these other verses in mind that we assert that the "purpose" of Romans 8:28 is surely God's purpose of election referred to in Romans 9:11.

These various Bible verses are a testimony to the truth that the Holy Spirit works in accordance with the purpose of the Father and the purchase of the Son in applying salvation to his people.

Faith is God's gift, worked by the Spirit

The faith by which the sinner is joined to Christ and justified before God, is God's gift to the sinner and is worked by the grace of the Holy Spirit (Ephesians 2:8,9; Acts 18:27; Philippians 1:29).

Note that the same thing is also said about repentance: Acts 5:31; 11:18; 2 Timothy 2:25. This does not mean that God repents and believes for the sinner. The sinner is the one who must repent and believe; but it simply explains to us that the sinner does this "through grace." The Spirit of God operating within that sinner enables him and gives him the ability to repent and believe. This is part of the work of effectual calling.

Acts 11:18
When they heard these things they became silent; and they glorified God, saying, "Then God has also granted to the Gentiles repentance to life."

2 Timothy 2:25
...in humility correcting those who are in opposition, if God perhaps will grant them repentance, so that they may know the truth.

In effectual calling the Holy Spirit reverses the terrible effects of the Fall

- he enlightens the mind (2 Corinthians 4:6)
- he re-orders the affections (Deuteronomy 30:6)
- he liberates the will (Psalm 110:3)

In doing these things and giving the grace of repentance and faith, the Holy Spirit

Psalm 110:3
Your people *shall be* volunteers In the day of Your power; In the beauties of holiness, from the womb of the morning, You have the dew of Your youth.

brings the sinner to a willing and joyful acceptance of Christ. The Holy Spirit does not deal with sinners as robots but as human beings. His work in them is always in harmony with their human "makeup." He does not force and coerce. Rather, he causes them to be willing.

This calling of the Spirit is a holy calling

See 2 Timothy 1:9.

1) *It is a calling unto holiness* (1 Thessalonians 4:7)

1 Thessalonians 4:7
For God did not call us to uncleanness, but in holiness.

2) *It is a calling out of darkness into light* (1 Peter 2:9)
3) *It is a calling to be saints* (Romans 1:7)
4) *It is a calling into the fellowship of Christ* (1 Corinthians 1:9)
5) *It is a calling to follow Christ's example* (1 Peter 1:21)

1 Peter 1:21
...who through Him believe in God, who raised Him from the dead and gave Him glory, so that your faith and hope are in God.

Those whom God hath accepted in the Beloved, effectually called and sanctified by his Spirit and given the precious faith of his Elect unto, can neither totally nor finally fall from the state of grace, but shall certainly persevere therein to the end and be eternally saved...

Second London Confession of Faith 17.1 (1689)

Through many dangers, toils, and snares
I have already come;
'Tis grace has brought me safe thus far
And grace will lead me home.

John Newton (1725–1807)
—from his hymn "Amazing Grace"

5 Explaining perseverance

Once having brought a person to walk the path of life in Christ, the path of faith, love, obedience and holiness, God will ensure that he continues in that way until God takes him home to glory.

The necessity of perseverance

1) *Perseverance in the faith is the acid test of Christian profession.*
   (John 8:31; Hebrews 3:12–14)
2) *Jesus declared that only those who persevered to the end would be saved.*
   (Matthew 24:13)
3) *Perseverance is that which distinguishes the genuine believer from the false professor.*
   (1 John 2:19)

There is such a thing as apostasy (Hebrews 6:1–9). In the light of what we shall consider below those who commit apostasy cannot have been truly in Christ in the first place. Remarkable religious experiences are not the real test of Christian profession. There is such a thing as false (temporary) faith (Matthew 13:20,21). But true saints will persevere for the reasons that follow.

John 8:31
Then Jesus said to those Jews who believed Him, "If you abide in My word, you are My disciples indeed."

Matthew 24:13
"But he who endures to the end shall be saved."

Romans 8:28
And we know that all things work together for good to those who love God, to those who are the called according to *His* purpose.

Isaiah 46:10,11
Declaring the end from the beginning, And from ancient times *things* that are not *yet* done, Saying, 'My counsel shall stand, And I will do all My pleasure,' Calling a bird of prey from the east, The man who executes My counsel, from a far country. Indeed I have spoken *it*; I will also bring it to pass. I have purposed *it*; I will also do it.

Romans 8:35–39
Who shall separate us from the love of Christ? *Shall* tribulation, or distress, or persecution, or famine, or nakedness, or peril, or sword? As it is written: "For Your sake we are killed all day long; We are accounted as sheep for the slaughter." Yet in all these things we are more than conquerors through Him who loved us. For I am persuaded that neither death nor life, nor angels nor principalities nor powers, nor things present nor things to come, nor height nor depth, nor any other created thing, shall be able to separate us from the love of God which is in Christ Jesus our Lord.

John 10:28
"And I give them eternal life, and they shall never perish; neither shall anyone snatch them out of My hand."

The purpose of God

The salvation of any person ultimately comes about because of the purpose of God. God's election is according to his purpose (Romans 9:11), and effectual calling is according to his purpose (Romans 8:28).

If a man's salvation is purposed therefore by God (Acts 13:48) that salvation will be effected, for God always fulfills his purposes (Isaiah 46:10,11; Daniel 4:35).

The power of God

In John 10 Jesus links the believer's security with both the purpose and the power of God (John 10:29). God describes himself as "Almighty God" (Genesis 17:1). Thus, we can rightly speak of him as the omnipotent God. His power extends over all things animate and inanimate. Because of this awesome power nothing can separate the believer from the love of God, as we read in Romans 8:35–39.

Perseverance rooted in the promises of God

God has promised that his people shall have everlasting life. He has promised that they will be "kept" and brought before his throne (John 5:24; 6:39; 10:28; Matthew 28:20; Titus 1:1,2).

God will not go back on his promises and he declares them to be "yea and amen" in Jesus Christ (2 Corinthians 1:20).

Perseverance secured by the prayers of Christ

The present ministry of Christ is that of intercession (Romans 8:34). For what is Christ praying right now? Read John 17:24. Note also Hebrews 7:25; this verse from the letter to the Hebrews is of great significance. It is not enough that we merely begin the Christian life, we must, as the nineteenth-century Baptist preacher, Charles Haddon Spurgeon says, "persevere or perish." We must be "saved to the uttermost"; to use the words of Hebrews 7, and that only comes about through the intercession of the living Christ.

Christ is praying that supplies of grace be given to his people, that they might persevere. He is praying that their faith shall not fail (Luke 22:32). And his prayer will be answered! For Christ's prayers are always granted by the Father (John 11:41,42).

John 17:24
"Father, I desire that they also whom You gave Me may be with Me where I am, that they may behold My glory which You have given Me; for You loved Me before the foundation of the world."

Perseverance found in the permanence of the Spirit's indwelling

The Spirit of God is given to every believer to be in him and to be with him forever (John 14:16,17; Ephesians 4:30). None who are the temples of the Holy Spirit will end up in hell.

John 14:16,17
"And I will pray the Father, and He will give you another Helper, that He may abide with you forever — the Spirit of truth, whom the world cannot receive, because it neither sees Him nor knows Him; but you know Him, for He dwells with you and will be in you."

But note what this doctrine does not mean

- It does not mean that so long as a person has "asked Jesus to come into his heart," that he is therefore saved even though his life is not in the least changed. We must understand that true faith always reveals

Ephesians 4:30
And do not grieve the Holy Spirit of God, by whom you were sealed for the day of redemption.

James 2:14–17
What *does it* profit, my brethren, if someone says he has faith but does not have works? Can faith save him? If a brother or sister is naked and destitute of daily food, and one of you says to them, "Depart in peace, be warmed and filled," but you do not give them the things which are needed for the body, what *does it* profit? Thus also faith by itself, if it does not have works, is dead.

Luke 22:31–34
And the Lord said, "Simon, Simon! Indeed, Satan has asked for you, that he may sift *you* as wheat. "But I have prayed for you, that your faith should not fail; and when you have returned to *Me*, strengthen your brethren." But he said to Him, "Lord, I am ready to go with You, both to prison and to death." Then He said, "I tell you, Peter, the rooster shall not crow this day before you will deny three times that you know Me."

1 Timothy 6:12
Fight the good fight of faith, lay hold on eternal life, to which you were also called and have confessed the good confession in the presence of many witnesses.

itself by works and spiritual fruit (James 2:14–17; 2 Corinthians 5:17; Matthew 7:21–23; Ephesians 2:8–10; 1 John 1:6; 2:3,4; 3:9,14,24; 5:2–4).

- It does not mean that a true Christian may not experience periods of backsliding and spiritual decline. Read about the Apostle Peter's experience in this regard in Luke 22:31–34.
- It does not mean that a Christian can sit back and do nothing about maintaining his spiritual ardour and passion, and will nevertheless be kept by God. Notice the "conflict" terminology of the New Testament (Ephesians 6:11–20; 1 Timothy 6:12; 2 Corinthians 10:4,5).

Those who are careless and indifferent to spiritual things and disobedient to the Lord Jesus Christ can take no comfort from this doctrine. It speaks of the *perseverance* (the ongoing walk in faith, love, obedience and holiness) of the *saints* (those who are separated or committed to Christ). The expression "once saved always saved" is true only as long as our understanding of "saved" is biblical. If it is not, then this popular expression can be highly dangerous and even fatal. Our forefathers were wiser in their terminology. For they spoke of "persevering in the faith."

But this doctrine is both a stimulus (they *must* persevere) and a comfort (they *shall* be preserved) to all true believers. Grace shall keep them, protect them, enable them, strengthen them, preserve them and ultimately bring them home to glory.

Regeneration is that act of God by which the principle of the new life is implanted in man, and the governing disposition of the soul is made holy, and the first holy exercise of this new disposition is secured.

Louis Berkhof (1873–1957)
—*from his* Systematic Theology

6 Exploring regeneration

The need for regeneration

Jesus plainly said "you must be born again" (John 3:7) and "unless one is born again he cannot see the kingdom of God" (John 3:3).

Why is this? Because of our condition "by nature": by nature we are "dead in trespasses and sins (Ephesians 2:1; compare also Colossians 2:13). Notice how this spiritual deadness expresses itself: "you once walked according to the course of this world, according to the prince of the power of the air, the spirit who now works in the sons of disobedience, among whom also we all once conducted ourselves in the lusts of our flesh, fulfilling the desires of the flesh and of the mind, and were by nature children of wrath, just as the others." (Ephesians 2:2,3).

What can a spiritually dead man do?

- he cannot receive the things of the Spirit (1 Corinthians 2:14)
- he cannot love and serve God (Romans 8:7,8)
- he cannot come to Christ (John 6:44)
- he is the slave of sin, under its domination and power (Romans 6:16–23; John 8:34)

Romans 6:16–23
Do you not know that to whom you present yourselves slaves to obey, you are that one's slaves whom you obey, whether of sin *leading* to death, or of obedience *leading* to righteousness? But God be thanked that *though* you were slaves of sin, yet you obeyed from the heart that form of doctrine to which you were delivered. And having been set free from sin, you became slaves of righteousness. I speak in human *terms* because of the weakness of your flesh. For just as you presented your members *as* slaves of uncleanness, and of lawlessness *leading* to *more* lawlessness, so now present your members *as* slaves *of* righteousness for holiness. For when you were slaves of sin, you were free in regard to righteousness. What fruit did you have then in the things of which you are now ashamed? For the end of those things *is* death. But now having been set free from sin, and having become slaves of God, you have your fruit to holiness, and the end, everlasting life. For the wages of sin *is* death, but the gift of God *is* eternal life in Christ Jesus our Lord.

These expressions do not mean that every person is totally debauched and wallowing in gross and flagrant sin. We may be quite cultured, well-mannered, educated and outwardly decent from a human perspective and yet be utterly dead spiritually and indifferent to the gospel. In fact, hostility to God is sometimes even cloaked by religion!

What does God do in regeneration?

What a spiritually dead person needs is spiritual life! Just as a person who is clinically dead on a hospital operating table can do absolutely nothing to bring himself back to life, but must rely on the medical intervention of the doctors, so it is the case with spiritual regeneration. God has to implant a new, living, holy principle within the soul of a dead sinner. This principle is:

- *new*, because it was not there before
- *living*, so that it will make its presence felt
- *holy*, for it will operate counter to sin and incline us to holiness and God.

Regeneration is a work of God in the soul unobserved by human eyes. It can be known, though, by its results and effects. God describes this work as the giving of a new heart and a new spirit in Ezekiel 36:25–27.

Ezekiel 36:31
"Then you will remember your evil ways and your deeds that *were* not good; and you will loathe yourselves in your own sight, for your iniquities and your abominations."

The results of regeneration

- recognition of our sinfulness and a humbling of ourselves (Ezekiel 36:31)
- a receptivity and sensitivity to the things

of God (Ezekiel 36:26)

- obedience to God, including a positive response to the gospel (Ezekiel 36:27)
- a new relationship with God (Ezekiel 36:28)

We may also observe the following:

- *faith in Christ* (1 John 5:1)
- *love for fellow Christians* (1 John 5:1)
- *not living in habitual sin* (1 John 3:9)
- *overcoming the world* (1 John 5:4)

Regeneration is the fountainhead from which the stream of sanctification flows. In regeneration there is the implanting of the spiritual life. In sanctification there is the developing and strengthening of it.

1 John 5:1
Whoever believes that Jesus is the Christ is born of God, and everyone who loves Him who begot also loves him who is begotten of Him.

Who is the agent in regeneration?

The Holy Spirit of God is the agent in regeneration: John 3:5. We cannot regenerate ourselves! The reference "water" in this verse is not a reference to baptism, but undoubtedly refers to the passage in Ezekiel 36 and has reference to the inner purification and cleansing of the heart that is part of the work of regeneration.

Remember that the Holy Spirit is the third person of the Holy Trinity. *He is not a force, but a person*:

- Jesus refers to the Holy Spirit as "he" (John 14:16,17)
- the Spirit expresses himself in Scripture (Hebrews 3:7–11)
- he exercises choice (1 Corinthians 12:11)

John 3:5
Jesus answered, "Most assuredly, I say to you, unless one is born of water and the Spirit, he cannot enter the kingdom of God."

Hebrews 3:7–11
Therefore, as the Holy Spirit says: "Today, if you will hear His voice, Do not harden your hearts as in the rebellion, In the day of trial in the wilderness, Where your fathers tested Me, tried Me, And saw My works forty years. Therefore I was angry with that generation, And said, 'They always go astray in *their* heart, And they have not known My ways.' So I swore in My wrath, 'They shall not enter My rest.' "

Ephesians 4:30
And do not grieve the Holy Spirit of God, by whom you were sealed for the day of redemption.

- he has a mind (1 Corinthians 2:11)
- he may be grieved and resisted (Ephesians 4:30; Acts 7:51)
- he loves (Romans 15:30)
- he may be lied to (Acts 5:3)

In the illustration of John 3:8 Jesus intimates two things. First, there is a mystery connected with the work of the Spirit. Second, there is sovereignty in the work of the Spirit. He works as he wills in regeneration. He quickens one yet not another.

John 8:32
"And you shall know the truth, and the truth shall make you free."

What is the instrument in regeneration?
The truth which makes us free (John 8:32). The Holy Spirit and the Word are like the surgeon and the instrument. You must have both for a successful operation.

Beware of error in this matter
Baptism cannot regenerate. No church ritual can regenerate. A human "decision" cannot regenerate. Responding to a so-called "altar-call" cannot regenerate. One may be religious, yet unregenerate—emotionally impacted by the truth of the gospel, yet unregenerate—knowledgeable about the Word of God, yet unregenerate.

Regeneration is a radical work. It affects the "heart," the "control centre" of the life. "You must be born again."

Justification is an act of God's free grace, wherein he pardons all our sins, and accepts us as righteous in his sight, only for the righteousness of Christ imputed to us, and received by faith alone.

Westminster Shorter Catechism (1647)
—answer to Question 33

7 Declaring justification

This is one of the most important doctrines in the Word of God. It was at the heart of the great Protestant Reformation in the sixteenth century. If we do not understand this doctrine we do not really understand the biblical Gospel.

Proverbs 17:15
He who justifies the wicked, and he who condemns the just,
Both of them alike *are* an abomination to the LORD.

Justification is concerned with our legal status, that is, our standing before God. The Greek word used in the New Testament for our word "justification" is from the language of the law courts. It refers to a declaration that a person is just, free from guilt and exposure to punishment.

It is sometimes said that justification is a declarative act of God, that is, it refers not to God doing something within a sinner (making him actually holy), but declaring something about the sinner, namely that he is accounted righteous.

For some Scripture references, see Deuteronomy 25:1; Proverbs 17:15; Isaiah 5:23; Luke 7:29; 16:15.

There are two elements in justification:

1) *Remission, that is, pardon.*
2) *Restoration to favour, that is, being accounted righteous.*

Zechariah 3:1–5
Then he showed me Joshua the high priest standing before the Angel of the LORD, and Satan standing at his right hand to oppose him. And the LORD said to Satan, "The LORD rebuke you, Satan! The LORD who has chosen Jerusalem rebuke you! *Is* this not a brand plucked from the fire?" Now Joshua was clothed with filthy garments, and was standing before the Angel. Then He answered and spoke to those who stood before Him, saying, "Take away the filthy garments from him." And to him He said, "See, I have removed your iniquity from you, and I will clothe you with rich robes." And I said, "Let them put a clean turban on his head." So they put a clean turban on his head, and they put the clothes on him. And the Angel of the LORD stood by.

Romans 8:33
Who shall bring a charge against God's elect? *It is* God who justifies.

Romans 5:8,9
But God demonstrates His own love toward us, in that while we were still sinners, Christ died for us. Much more then, having now been justified by His blood, we shall be saved from wrath through Him.

Note how these two elements are symbolically presented in Zechariah 3:1–5.

The One who justifies

The one who justifies is God (Romans 8:33). This is important for God is "the supreme court," so to speak. There is no appeal from his judgement. His word is final and authoritative.

The subjects of justification

The same people are described in a number of ways:

- God's elect (Romans 8:33)
- the ungodly (Romans 4:5)
- sinners (Romans 5:8,9)
- all who believe (Acts 13:38,39; Romans 4:5; 5:1; Galatians 2:16)

The ground or basis of justification

The blood and righteousness of Jesus Christ is the basis of the sinner's justification. This is sometimes referred to as the "obedience" of Christ. God is able to declare the believing sinner to be righteous because he imputes (for the terms "imputation" and "imputes" see the next paragraph) the obedience of Christ to the believer. It is on account of that imputed obedience that God can declare a sinner to be righteous (Romans 3:24,25; 5:8,9,16–19; 1 Corinthians 1:30; 2 Corinthians 5:21; Philippians 3:9).

To impute means to reckon, to credit, to

put to someone's account. Romans 4:6–8 speaks of a "non-imputation" of sin and an imputation of righteousness. The gospel is therefore a message about "provided righteousness"—God providing us a righteousness achieved by the spotless, holy life of Jesus Christ (Romans 1:17; 3:21,22). It is in this sense that we can call Jesus Christ "The Lord our Righteousness," a title drawn from Jeremiah 23:6.

Philippians 3:9
...and be found in Him, not having my own righteousness, which *is* from the law, but that which *is* through faith in Christ, the righteousness which is from God by faith.

Galatians 2:16
"knowing that a man is not justified by the works of the law but by faith in Jesus Christ, even we have believed in Christ Jesus, that we might be justified by faith in Christ and not by the works of the law; for by the works of the law no flesh shall be justified.

The means of justification

The means of justification is faith in Christ alone (Galatians 2:16; 3:8; Romans 3:28; 4:5; 5:1)

Note: Faith is not meritorious in itself. Its value lies wholly in the fact that it lays hold of Jesus Christ. Faith is the instrument by which the sinner receives and applies Christ and his righteousness to himself. It is not faith that saves him, but Christ made his *through* faith.

Romans 3:28
Therefore we conclude that a man is justified by faith apart from the deeds of the law.

Romans 5:1,2
Therefore, having been justified by faith, we have peace with God through our Lord Jesus Christ, through whom also we have access by faith into this grace in which we stand, and rejoice in hope of the glory of God.

The evidence of justification

Good works are the evidence of justification. (James 2:14–24; Ephesians 2:9,10). Contrary to what is sometimes argued, James and Paul are not in opposition to each other in the question of justification. They are dealing with different enemies. Paul is dealing with the person who insists that he may be justified by the works of the law. James is dealing with the man who claims he has justifying faith, but whose life is devoid of the fruits of it, namely good works.

James 2:14–24
What *does it* profit, my brethren, if someone says he has faith but does not have works? Can faith save him? If a brother or sister is naked and destitute of daily food, and one of you says to them, "Depart in peace, be warmed and filled," but you do not give them the things which are needed for the body, what *does it* profit? Thus also faith by itself, if it does not have works, is dead. But someone will say, "You have faith, and I have works." Show me your faith without your works, and I will show you my faith by my works. You believe that there is one God. You do well. Even the demons believe — and tremble! But do you want to know, O foolish man, that faith without works is dead? Was not Abraham our father justified by works when he offered Isaac his son on the altar? Do you see that faith was working together with his works, and by works faith was made perfect? And the Scripture was fulfilled which says, "Abraham believed God, and it was accounted to him for righteousness." And he was called the friend of God. You see then that a man is justified by works, and not by faith only.

The results of justification

- freedom from condemnation (Romans 8:1,33)
- peace with God (Romans 5:1)
- access to God (Romans 5:2)
- acceptance of our persons (Romans 8:33,34)
- title to eternal inheritance (Titus 3:5–7)
- eventual glorification (Romans 8:30)

There are no degrees in justification. No believer is more justified than any other. Justification is irreversible, unalterable, immediate (upon the sinner believing on Christ), and forever. All believers share this common blessing.[1]

The practical value of the doctrine of justification

1) *It tells us how we may have peace with God.*
2) *It is the foundation of all assurance.*
3) *It is the foundation of true, spiritual, Christian unity.*
4) *It moves the heart with admiration for God and with love and praise for such a great salvation.*

1 For the difference between justification and sanctification and the connection between them, see Chapter 8.

Sanctification is the work of God's free grace, whereby we are renewed in the whole man after the image of God, and are enabled more and more to die unto sin, and live unto righteousness.

Westminster Shorter Catechism (1647)
—answer to Question 35

Sanctification is that continuous operation of the Holy Spirit, by which the holy disposition imparted in regeneration is maintained and strengthened.

A.H. Strong (1836–1921)
—from his Systematic Theology

8 Experiencing sanctification

In justification the believer is *declared* by God to be righteous (see the previous chapter on justification). In sanctification the believer is *actually made to be holy* by God. We may say then that although justification has to do with our *standing* in the sight of God, sanctification has to do with our actual *state.*

1 Thessalonians 5:23
Now may the God of peace Himself sanctify you completely; and may your whole spirit, soul, and body be preserved blameless at the coming of our Lord Jesus Christ.

Sanctification—justification—regeneration

These three vital elements of the great work of salvation are intrinsically related. We may view justification as the foundation of the Christian life and sanctification as the superstructure. You cannot think of one without the other. Sanctification is the evidence of justification. To claim to be justified without giving evidence of sanctification is a delusion and a sham.

We may also say that regeneration is foundational to both of these. There can be no justification without regeneration, for faith (through which we are justified) is the action of the new heart given in regeneration. Likewise, there can be no sanctification without regeneration, because sanctification is but the strengthening and increasing of that holy principle imparted to the soul at regeneration. You cannot be sanctified (made holy) in the biblical sense, therefore, without being born again. You may well be moral or religious without regeneration, but you cannot be holy.

The author of sanctification

God himself is the author of sanctification (1 Thessalonians 5:23; 2 Thessalonians 2:13; John 17:17). In particular, it is God the Holy Spirit who makes men holy (Romans 8:13; Galatians 5:16; Ephesians 5:18).

The standard of sanctification

This may be expressed in a variety of ways:

- God the Father (Matthew 5:48; 1 Peter 1:15,16)
- the Lord Jesus Christ (Romans 8:29)
- the revealed will of God in Scripture (Romans 12:1,2)

The fact that perfection cannot be attained in this life ought not to keep us from making perfection our constant aim.

The means of sanctification

- faith in the Lord Jesus Christ (Acts 15:9)
- the Word of God (John 17:17; Acts 20:32)
- prayer (Psalm 51:10; Jude 20)
- Christian fellowship (Hebrews 10:24,25; Proverbs 13:20)
- providential experiences (Psalm 119:67,71)

Romans 8:13
For if you live according to the flesh you will die; but if by the Spirit you put to death the deeds of the body, you will live.

Romans 12:1,2
I beseech you therefore, brethren, by the mercies of God, that you present your bodies a living sacrifice, holy, acceptable to God, *which is* your reasonable service. And do not be conformed to this world, but be transformed by the renewing of your mind, that you may prove what *is* that good and acceptable and perfect will of God.

Jude 20
But you, beloved, building yourselves up on your most holy faith, praying in the Holy Spirit.

Proverbs 13:20
He who walks with wise *men* will be wise, But the companion of fools will be destroyed.

Psalm 119:67,71
Before I was afflicted I went astray, But now I keep Your word....*It is* good for me that I have been afflicted, That I may learn Your statutes.

The necessity of sanctification

- without it no man shall see the Lord (Hebrews 12:14)
- by it we bring glory to God (Matthew 5:16)
- by it we are a witness to others (Philippians 2:12–16; Titus 3:8)

The Christian's responsibility in sanctification

Though sanctification is a work of God, yet he involves the Christian in it. The Christian is not passive but active in this great work. Carefully note the involvement of God in sanctifying the believer and the exhortation to the believer to press after holiness in Philippians 2:12,13. In sanctification the Christian is to:

- exercise discipline over himself (1 Corinthians 9:25–27)
- put forth effort (2 Corinthians 7:1; Hebrews 12:14)
- fight (1 Timothy 6:12)
- run the race of the Christian life (Hebrews 12:1)

We must recognize of course that our effort is not to be rooted in self-confidence, but in complete dependence on God (Romans 8:13; Philippians 4:13).

Sanctification is incomplete in this life

Though it affects every part of our life (1 Thessalonians 5:23), yet it is not complete (Philippians 3:12–15; 1 John 1:7–9; 3:2,3).

Hebrews 12:14
Pursue peace with all *people*, and holiness, without which no one will see the Lord.

Philippians 2:12,13
Therefore, my beloved, as you have always obeyed, not as in my presence only, but now much more in my absence, work out your own salvation with fear and trembling; for it is God who works in you both to will and to do for *His* good pleasure.

1 Timothy 6:12
Fight the good fight of faith, lay hold on eternal life, to which you were also called and have confessed the good confession in the presence of many witnesses.

Philippians 3:12–15
Not that I have already attained, or am already perfected; but I press on, that I may lay hold of that for which Christ Jesus has also laid hold of me. Brethren, I do not count myself to have apprehended; but one thing *I do*, forgetting those things which are behind and reaching forward to those things which are ahead, I press toward the goal for the prize of the upward call of God in Christ Jesus. Therefore let us, as many as are mature, have this mind; and if in anything you think otherwise, God will reveal even this to you.

Philippians 1:9–11
And this I pray, that your love may abound still more and more in knowledge and all discernment, that you may approve the things that are excellent, that you may be sincere and without offense till the day of Christ, being filled with the fruits of righteousness which *are* by Jesus Christ, to the glory and praise of God.

Sanctification is progressive in nature

- Biblical figures of speech indicate this (compared to development from babyhood to adulthood)
  (Hebrews 5:12–14; 1 Peter 2:1,2; Ephesians 4:14,15)
- Biblical exhortations imply this
  (2 Peter 1:5–8; 3:18)
- the prayers of Paul for his converts reveal this (Colossians 1:9,11; Philippians 1:9–11)
- the general teaching of the New Testament states this (2 Corinthians 3:18; 7:1; Romans 12:2)

Some attempted substitutes for sanctification

- morality
- religious ritual
- hypocrisy

For the sake of his only Son, Jesus Christ, God has been pleased to make all justified persons sharers in the grace of adoption, by means of which they are numbered with, and enjoy the liberties and privileges of children of God. Furthermore, God's name is put upon them, they receive the Spirit of adoption, and they are enabled to come boldly to the throne of grace and cry 'Abba, Father.' They are pitied, protected, provided for, and chastened by God as by a Father. He never casts them off, but, as they remain sealed to the day of redemption, they inherit the promises as heirs of everlasting salvation.

A Faith to Confess: The Baptist Confession of Faith of 1689 —Chapter 12

9 The privilege of adoption

J.I. Packer calls adoption "the highest privilege the gospel offers."[1] A little thought will confirm this statement. It is one thing to be forgiven of our sins and acquitted at the bar of the Great Judge; that is wonderful in itself. But it is even more wonderful to be made a member of God's family, established as a son or daughter and given all the privileges of God's children.

1 John 3:1,2
Behold what manner of love the Father has bestowed on us, that we should be called children of God! Therefore the world does not know us, because it did not know Him. Beloved, now we are children of God; and it has not yet been revealed what we shall be, but we know that when He is revealed, we shall be like Him, for we shall see Him as He is.

The cause of our adoption from the divine perspective

From God's vantage-point the predestinating purpose of God is the cause of our adoption (Ephesians 1:5). Note that this verse tells us adoption is "by Jesus Christ." It is "according to the good pleasure of his will." And ultimately it is "to the praise of the glory of His grace" (Ephesians 1:6a).

Adoption again has as its root cause the wonderful love of God (1 John 3:1,2).

The cause of our adoption from the human perspective

From the human side, our adoption is rooted in faith in the Lord Jesus Christ (John

[1] *Knowing God* (Downers Grove, Illinois: InterVarsity Press, 1973), 186.

1:12,13; Galatians 3:26)

Galatians 4:6
And because you are sons, God has sent forth the Spirit of His Son into your hearts, crying out, "Abba, Father!"

Romans 8:14,15
For as many as are led by the Spirit of God, these are sons of God. For you did not receive the spirit of bondage again to fear, but you received the Spirit of adoption by whom we cry out, "Abba, Father."

The great initial blessing of adoption

The gift of the Holy Spirit is the great initial blessing that comes with adoption (Galatians 4:6; Romans 8:15).

The Holy Spirit produces in the Christian the consciousness of God as Father. This is a revelation that is unique to the new covenant proclaimed by Christ and expounded in the New Testament. In the Old Testament the emphasis is on God as Creator, the Sovereign Lord, the Holy and Just One. These emphases remain in the New Testament, but to them is added the new and wonderful dimension that God is the Father of his people (Matthew 6:9). This was the name most frequently on the lips of our Lord. It is the distinctive Christian name for God. And all that the name "Father" implies in the way of love, affection, tenderness, care, provision, fellowship and guidance is to be understood in this wonderful name.

Further blessings of adoption

- adopted sons are led by the Spirit (Romans 8:14)
- they are free from bondage and fear (Romans 8:15)
- they are assured of ultimate complete conformity to Christ (1 John 3:2; Romans 8:29)

Some ramifications of our adoption

- we must seek to imitate the Heavenly Father (Matthew 5:43–48)
- we must be overcomers (Revelation 21:7)
- we must not partake of the world's defilement (2 Corinthians 6:14–18)
- we must expect the Father's discipline (Hebrews 12:4–11)

The extraordinary privilege of our adoption

- we are made heirs of God (Romans 8:17; Hebrews 1:2; 1 Corinthians 3:21–23)
- we are given an inheritance (Ephesians 1:11; 1 Peter 1:3,4)

The practical effects of this doctrine of adoption

1) *It gives us a powerful view of the depths of God's love and grace, and should therefore produce love, praise and gratitude in us.*
2) *It should challenge us to live as children of the King.*
3) *It should give us confidence in our dealings with God.*
4) *It gives us encouragement in times of suffering.*
5) *It breaks down barriers among Christians.*
6) *It gives us hope and assurance for the future.*

Once we are members of God's family by grace we can never cease to be members of that family. We may lose the Father's favour through our sin and unfaithfulness, and we may lose the joy and blessing of fellowship with him, but we remain children of God in

Matthew 5:43–48
" You have heard that it was said, 'You shall love your neighbor and hate your enemy.' But I say to you, love your enemies, bless those who curse you, do good to those who hate you, and pray for those who spitefully use you and persecute you, that you may be sons of your Father in heaven; for He makes His sun rise on the evil and on the good, and sends rain on the just and on the unjust. For if you love those who love you, what reward have you? Do not even the tax collectors do the same? And if you greet your brethren only, what do you do more *than others*? Do not even the tax collectors do so? Therefore you shall be perfect, just as your Father in heaven is perfect."

1 Peter 1:3,4
Blessed *be* the God and Father of our Lord Jesus Christ, who according to His abundant mercy has begotten us again to a living hope through the resurrection of Jesus Christ from the dead, to an inheritance incorruptible and undefiled and that does not fade away, reserved in heaven for you.

Christ. He will chastise us for our sins in order to renew us to fellowship, but he will not disown his children. But it should ever be the aim of God's children to please the Father and to know the blessing of unbroken fellowship with him.

Face to face with Christ my Saviour,
Face to face—what will it be,
When with rapture I behold Him,
Jesus Christ who died for me?

Carrie E. Breck (1855–1934)
—from her hymn "Face to Face"

When I stand before the throne,
Dressed in beauty not my own,
When I see Thee as Thou art,
Love Thee with unsinning heart,
Then Lord shall I fully know,
Not till then how much I owe.

Robert Murray M'Cheyne (1813–1843)
—from his hymn "When this passing world is done"

Then He will own my worthless name
Before His Father's face;
And in the new Jerusalem
Appoint my soul a place.

Isaac Watts (1674–1748)
—from his hymn "I'm not ashamed to own my Lord"

10 The hope of glorification

Glorification is the ultimate goal of salvation: Romans 8:17,30. Notice in these verses the way that Paul speaks of it as though it were already accomplished. The glorification of believers will be brought about at the second coming of the Lord Jesus Christ (2 Thessalonians 1:6–10).

The second coming of Christ is certain—John 14:3; Matthew 24:30, 25:31. It will be:

- personal (1 Thessalonians 4:16)
- visible (Revelation 1:7)
- glorious (Mark 13:26).

It will catch many by surprise (1 Thessalonians 5:2,3). And, it will mark the end of time and usher in the eternal state. For this last point, read the entirety of 2 Peter 3.

The following six elements may be considered as belonging to the believer's glorification:

1) *Resurrection*

This refers to the raising up of the dead and the transforming of their bodies. This stupendous truth is insisted on by the Lord Jesus and the New Testament writers: John 5:28–30; 6:39,40. Paul insists that the resurrection of believers is the inevitable outcome of Christ's

Revelation 1:7
Behold, He is coming with clouds, and every eye will see Him, even they who pierced Him. And all the tribes of the earth will mourn because of Him. Even so, Amen.

Mark 13:26
"Then they will see the Son of Man coming in the clouds with great power and glory."

1 Thessalonians 5:2,3
For you yourselves know perfectly that the day of the Lord so comes as a thief in the night. For when they say, "Peace and safety!" then sudden destruction comes upon them, as labor pains upon a pregnant woman. And they shall not escape.

1 Corinthians 15:20,22
But now Christ is risen from the dead, *and* has become the firstfruits of those who have fallen asleep....For as in Adam all die, even so in Christ all shall be made alive.

1 Corinthians 15:42–44
So also *is* the resurrection of the dead. *The body* is sown in corruption, it is raised in incorruption. It is sown in dishonor, it is raised in glory. It is sown in weakness, it is raised in power. It is sown a natural body, it is raised a spiritual body. There is a natural body, and there is a spiritual body.

resurrection (1 Corinthians 15:20,22; 1 Thessalonians 4:14–16).

Believers who are living at the time of Christ's return will not see death, but shall be transformed, as taught in 1 Corinthians 15:51,52.

The resurrection body will be glorious indeed. It will be:

- not subject to death, decay or corruption (1 Corinthians 15:42,43,52,53)
- a perfect vehicle for the perfected spirit (1 Corinthians 15:44)
- fitted for eternity (1 Thessalonians 4:17)
- possessed of powers and abilities very different from our present body. See, for instance, the activity of Christ after his resurrection, as found in texts like Luke 24:13–16,30,31,36; John 20:19,26.
- conformed to Christ's glorious resurrection body (1 Corinthians 15:49; Philippians 3:21)

2) *The beholding of our beloved Lord and Saviour*
Glorification will mean seeing our dear Lord and Saviour in his risen, glorified humanity: Isaiah 33:17; Job 19:25–27; 1 John 3:1,2.

John 17:24
"Father, I desire that they also whom You gave Me may be with Me where I am, that they may behold My glory which You have given Me; for You loved Me before the foundation of the world."

Of all the things the saints long for they long for most to see Jesus and to behold His glory (John 17:24).

3) *Total perfection*

- freedom from all sin (Romans 8:29) in word, thought and deed
- "We shall be like him" (1 John 3:2; compare Revelation 21:22–27). What a

thought!

- freedom from all sorrow and pain (Revelation 21:4; Psalm 16:11)
- confirmation in holiness for ever (Revelation 22:11)

4) *Unending and unbroken fellowship with God*

Revelation 21:1–3 and 22:3–5 depict this fellowship beautifully.

5) *The acknowledgement of believers as the children of God*

On the anticipation of this, see Hebrews 2:10–13; 11:16; Matthew 10:32.

6) *The enjoyment of an environment suited to a glorified state*

2 Peter 3:13 puts this well when it states: "according to His promise, look for new heavens and a new earth in which righteousness dwells." The new heavens and the new earth will be a place where the righteous, God's children, are completely at home.

Applicatory thoughts

- how magnificent is God's purpose in salvation!
- what a future the Christian has to look forward to!
- what madness it is to turn away from such blessings!
- here is a truth to give us songs in the night!

Revelation 21:22–27
But I saw no temple in it, for the Lord God Almighty and the Lamb are its temple. The city had no need of the sun or of the moon to shine in it, for the glory of God illuminated it. The Lamb *is* its light. And the nations of those who are saved shall walk in its light, and the kings of the earth bring their glory and honor into it. Its gates shall not be shut at all by day (there shall be no night there). And they shall bring the glory and the honor of the nations into it. But there shall by no means enter it anything that defiles, or causes an abomination or a lie, but only those who are written in the Lamb's Book of Life.

Revelation 21:1–3
Now I saw a new heaven and a new earth, for the first heaven and the first earth had passed away. Also there was no more sea. Then I, John, saw the holy city, New Jerusalem, coming down out of heaven from God, prepared as a bride adorned for her husband. And I heard a loud voice from heaven saying, "Behold, the tabernacle of God *is* with men, and He will dwell with them, and they shall be His people. God Himself will be with them *and be* their God.

"Even so, come Lord Jesus"
(Revelation 22:20)

Further reading

An excellent development of the material found in the first five chapters of this book is found in John Cheeseman, *Saving Grace* (Edinburgh: Banner of Truth Trust, 1999), which first appeared as *The Grace of God in the Gospel* (Edinburgh: Banner of Truth Trust, 1972). Also helpful on the topic of election and predestination is R.C. Sproul, *Chosen by God* (Wheaton, Illinois: Tyndale House Publishers, Inc., 1986). The undisputed classic defence of particular redemption is still John Owen's *The Death of Death in the Death of Christ* in *The Works of John Owen*, ed. Willliam H. Goold (1850–1853 ed.; repr. Edinburgh: Banner of Truth Trust, 1967), X, 139–479, which is also published as a separate volume by the Banner of Truth with a noteworthy introduction by J.I. Packer. For a modernized, abridged and easy-to-read version of this work by Owen, see *Life By His Death*, abridged H.J. Appleby (London: Grace Publications Trust, 1992).

For a study of regeneration that ties this biblical truth into the larger framework of Christian theology, see A.T.B. McGowan, *The New Birth* (Fearn, Ross-shire: Christian Focus,

1996). Also see J.I. Packer, "Regeneration" in his *God's Words: Studies of Key Bible Themes* (Downers Grove, Illinois: InterVarsity Press, 1981), 148–155. A classic exposition of the doctrine of justification can be found in Jonathan Edwards, *Justification by Faith Alone*, ed. Don Kistler (Morgan, Pennsylvania: Soli Deo Gloria Publications, 2000). This book is comprised of sermons that Edwards preached in November, 1734, and which, in the hands of the Spirit of God, were a catalyst for revival in that town the following month through to June 1735.

For a solidly biblical study of the topic of sanctification, the reader should consult Kenneth Prior, *The Way of Holiness: A Study in Christian Growth* (Downers Grove, Illinois: InterVarsity Press, 1982). Prior's study is balanced, stressing both the Holy Spirit's sovereignty in the work of sanctification as well as the believer's responsibility to exercise active obedience to the will of God. J.I. Packer has a number of helpful studies on the subject of sanctification, among them "Predestination and Sanctification," which was first published in the July 1983 issue of *Tenth*, the magazine of Tenth Presbyterian Church. It can also be found in *The Collected Shorter Writings of J.I. Packer: Volume 2: Serving the People of God* (Carlisle, Cumbria: Paternoster Press, 1988), 317–327.

Finally, for a fine, systematic study of most of the subjects of this book, see Robert L.

Reymond, *A New Systematic Theology of the Christian Faith* (Nashville: Thomas Nelson Publishers, 1998), 703–801.

Michael A.G. Haykin
January 2001

Other titles available from Joshua Press

Classics of Reformed Spirituality series

The revived Puritan:
The spirituality of George Whitefield

ISBN 1-894400-06-2

Edited and introduced
by Michael A.G. Haykin

George Whitefield was a man of uncommon piety and holiness. He was used by God in a powerful way in the eighteenth century to bring about true revival in England and America. Dr. Haykin writes an engaging introduction to *The revived Puritan* which focuses on Whitefield's walk with God and his deep experience of the new birth. The selections from Whitefield's letters which follow, many unpublished since the eighteenth century, provide a first-hand look at his spirituality and are a source of meditation, encouragement and challenge for those seeking revival and spiritual awakening in our day.

256 pages, 4-1/4" x 7" smyth sewn, softcover

"To honour God":
The spirituality of Oliver Cromwell

ISBN 1-894400-03-8

Edited and introduced
by Michael A.G. Haykin

Michael Haykin provides an introduction and brief study of Cromwell's spirituality through a consideration of his view of divine providence, conversion and activism. A chronology of the life of Cromwell is followed by 30 selections from his letters, speeches, sayings and prayers. These selections are footnoted with interesting historical detail and include relevant biblical references.

136 pages, 4-1/4" x 7" smyth sewn, softcover

Led by the Spirit:

How the Holy Spirit guides the believer

ISBN 1-894400-00-3

by Jim Elliff

What does it mean to follow God? In a personal and pastoral way, Jim Elliff seeks to help the believer gain confidence in understanding and following the will of God. This book is not only practical, but answers some of the most important questions which confuse sincere believers in their desire to do God's will. Jim Elliff emphasizes that guidance has far more to do with sanctified reason than such extraordinary measures as seeing signs or hearing voices. This is a balanced and biblical approach to a vital subject.

48 pages, 4-1/4" x 7" smyth sewn, softcover

Heavenly fire:

The life and ministry of William Grimshaw of Haworth

ISBN 1-894400-08-9

by Esther Bennett

Though little known today, William Grimshaw was a powerful force in the Evangelical Revival in the north of England in the eighteenth-century. Under his tireless ministry, hundreds in the town of Haworth and the surrounding vicinity came to know Christ. Esther Bennett writes an engaging overview of his life and ministry which will inspire and encourage today's readers in what God can do in the hearts of men and women through His word and the power of His Spirit.

24 pages, 8" x 8" saddle-stitch, colour, softcover

A foundation for life

A study of key Christian doctrines and their application

ISBN 1-894400-17-8

Edited by Michael A.G. Haykin

In this book, we have brought together some contemporary pastors and church leaders to help explain the basic doctrines of the Christian faith in an easy, understandable way. After all, throughout history, the Bible has provided the surest foundation for living that this world can offer!

140 pages, 6" x 9", softcover

Deo Optimo et Maximo Gloria
To God, best and greatest, be glory

Cover and book design by Janice Van Eck
Set in Stone Sans and Stone Serif

CPSIA information can be obtained at www.ICGtesting.com
Printed in the USA
LVOW13s1834121213

365049LV00003B/544/A